FAIRY TAIL

Chapter 75:
Dream of a Butterfly

You're a celestial spirit?!!!

!!?

Neither is Virgo. You know her. She looks just like a regular girl, right?

Hold it a second! You aren't a cow or a horse or anything!

I never even guessed.

STARE

STARE

Well, I guess it boils down to that.

STARE

STARE

Lion?!!!

Loke is from the Lion Palace.

Now that you mention it, I guess you're right.

Nope! She can also look like a huge gorilla!

Hey, that's cool!

Come to think of it, you still look exactly the same. There's no problem with that?

Lion... Isn't that like a grown-up cat?

Exactly.

Exactly wrong!!!

I have to be Lucy's knight in shining armor, appearing to rescue her whenever she's in danger.

It might not be possible from now on. Lucy is my owner now, and I'm at her bidding.

Must be nice, huh? I want a celestial spirit of my own!

Huh? What kind of spirit?

Hey! Put me down!!

And thus, we head off to discuss our future in depth.

You can go home now.

Absolutely true! Celestial spirits are meant for love!

PWIK

Celestial wizards don't use their spirits as punching bags or sparring partners!!

Here I am, knowing everything a guy needs to know to be a dragon slayer! But what's the point if I don't have a dragon to fight with?!

A dragon!! What else?!!

SHH SHH

SHH SHH SHH

Here!

FLIP

SHH

Wait just a minute!

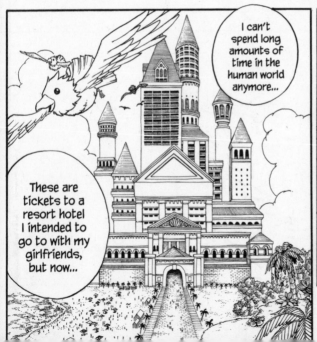

I can't spend long amounts of time in the human world anymore...

These are tickets to a resort hotel I intended to go to with my girlfriends, but now...

What are these?

Gray-sama! You're so fearless...

Ahh! ♡

Gray, why don't we put on some swim trunks, okay?

Wow!!! This is great!!!

Look at this!! This water is crystal clear!!!

SPLOOSH

All right!

LAP

Up! Up!

Right! Right!

What do you mean, "up?!"

More to your left!

WAVER

There !!!

WAVER

It was a very enjoyable day...

Truly...

Erza...
Freedom does not
exist in this world!

!!!

WHOOSH

A dream...?

....

KACHIK

I fell asleep without realizing it.

RATTLE

RATTLE

It's true. I just feel more at ease in armor.

Heh heh... I guess there is no help for a woman like me.

FOO

OOM

Erza!!!!

When I have the freedom to treat myself well.

It's all right to do this every now and again.

PHOOO

PHOOO

PHOOO

PHWOOOOO

Nothing is "making" it come out, sir!

It went into number 17, but something made it come out again! What kind of place is this?!!

Even so, it isn't allowed...

Aye!

It went into number 17!!! I saw it!!!

Excuse me, sir. But you're not allowed to do that.

Hm?

Gray-sama?

Ha ha! Look at the hopeless loser!

Y-You... You're...

BWAHAA?

GWAAA

BWOOOM

Juvia decided to come, too.

Wha?!!

Heh!

Wh-What do you think you're doing?!!

AAAAHH

Eeeee!!!

He's got a gun!!!

Va...

Vag's viz dis jawk?!

Juvia wants to join!

Ack! Don't tell me you want to join Fairy Tail?

But with the stuff you guys did... I don't mind if you join, but I wonder what the Master will say...

Now Juvia has become a free wizard.

GLEAM
GLEAM
GLEAM
GLEAM
GLEAM

Yes.

I heard Phantom's been disbanded, huh?

DWAAAAAAAAAN

Huh...? Wait a minute...

New dealer.

Heh heh... Luck is with me tonight.

GWIP

You're incredible, Erza!!!

And we won't simply be betting for a few coins.

If so, then shall we play a special game?

Darn straight!

I'm afraid there is no dealer who can change my luck now.

!

SHFF

SHFF

SHFF

Let's gamble...

...a life.

Big Sister Erza!

Shô...

......

?

26

FAIRY TAIL

Chapter 76:
The Tower of Heaven

CHATTER CHATTER CHATTER

CHATTER CHATTER

Shô...

Long time, no see...

...Big Sis.

Huh?

Huh?

Ah... No, I mean...

Okay?

So you...

...are all right...

You will not lay a finger on Gray-sama!

Juvia will take you on!!

There is danger gathering...

...around Erza!

Juvia...

So...

...I can just do the clean up, huh?

Oh! Fine.

You already found her?

!

BZZT

Hm?

BUMP

!!!

BWAAAH

Right!

It's Magic of the Dark Lineage.

The Black Moment!!!

!!!

JATTER

Wh-What's going on here?!!

Huh?!

JATTER

Natsu!! Where are you?!!

Gnere arr you, Haffy?!!

Gn-Gnat's haffenig...

...dis dime?!!

GWAAH!!

GANCH

KRAK

Kyaaa!!

Natsu!!!

BLAM

Good night, boy!

FSH HHH HH

!!

The light is coming back...

!!!

BWAAAH

What's all this darkness about?!

Something's wrong...

Shô...

DEATH

Magic
?!

I'm able to
use magic
now, too.

HEH
HEH
HEH...

You...?
How...?

Myaa
!!

FLIK FLIK

You can use magic, too?!

Millian-na?!

What are you doing?! Lucy is a friend of mine!!!

Er-chan! It's been a long time!!

Big Sis?!

But *we* were your friends, weren't we?

Myaa?

"Friend"?

Urk...

True...

They're her...old friends?

The only way to be a dandy is to keep your emotions in check! Get it?

VEET VEET

?!

Now don't go playing dirty tricks on Erza, Shô!

VEET VEET VEET

I- I know that voice... Wally?

Eee !!!

Look at you!! Getting all sexy on us!!

POHHH

Why are you so surprised?

You've got magic, too...?

RATTLE RATTLE

I don't blame you for not realizing it was me right away. Compared to when I was known as "Mad Dog Wally," I'm far more *well rounded!!!*

Anybody can do magic once you get the knack!

BWOOO

Isn't that right, Erza?!

Simon?!

Why did he call you his sister?!

Erza... Who are these people?!

Uff!!

WHUMP

Because I'm her little brother.

And we were once close friends!

GM GM GM GM GM

Why are you guys here?

Let Lucy go... please?

They're... talking about before that.

Friends?! Erza has been at Fairy Tail ever since she was little, right?!

Let's go home, Sis!

Myaa!

We're here to bring you home! Get it?

N- No!!

I'm begging you!! Please don't!!

GACHAK

Eeee!!!

And if you don't do like we say...

Chapter 77:
Jellal

Ungaaahh!!

STRUGGLE

STRUGGLE

Urngg!!

STRUGGLE

O-Open... Door to the great...

Crab Palace...!

CHANK

ROLL

ROLL

WHUMP

WHUMP

Taurus!!! Loke!!! Come out!!!

Cancer!!!

H-Huh?

Angah !!!

It's getting tighter and tighter...

Urgg !!

I... can't... ...use my magic ?!

?!

Ah! Ahh, sorry!

OWW !!

SLISS

Kyaaaaa!!!!

PAKIKK

KRAKL KRAKL

KRAKL

Huh?!

CHIKK

CHIKK

SHH SHH SHH

Eee!!!

SHH SHH SHH

You can relax!

SHHHHHHH

I-It's you?!!

Gray-sama is here within Juvia!

GAAHH!!

KAFF

KAFF

PSSHAAAA

WHLID

Y-Yeah... I know...

Not inside *you!* Inside Juvia!!

Ah ha...

Ah ha ha...

I-Inside...

And that interference let the guy get away!!

And Juvia put Gray in a water lock to be sure the enemy didn't find out!!

...so I figured I'd create a decoy of myself and check the situation, but...

It suddenly became pitch dark...

GONNG

Jellal-sama!

We've received word that Erza's capture was a success.

And that they are headed this way.

But...why would you want that traitor now?

That would never do.

Ha ha ha!

Ha ha...

For a man of your magical prowess, it should be easy work to finish her off.

HEH

This world is simply no fun!!

The time has come!

...it would only cause problems if we allowed her to live any longer.

However, now that the Tower of Heaven is complete...

?

Sir?

You will become a sacrifice upon the altar of my ambition...

...Erza Scarlet!!!

Jellal

Mm...

!!!

Inside the hold of a boat, Sis.

Shô!

Kh!

Where am I?!

GRNN

......

A boat?

I see...

So that's how it is...

Exactly. A boat bound for the Tower of Heaven.

Kh!!

GRNN

GRNN

You see, Sis... You're a traitor.

Not possible, I'm afraid.

Could you untie me? I have no intention of resisting.

No wizard can do anything while bound by them. Not even you.

Don't even try. Millianna's Tubes seal your magic away.

I'm frightened...

I don't want to go back to the tower...

A-All right... At the very least, can you let me requip into my armor?

But you look lovely in that dress, Sis.

If I'm not wearing my armor...

...I can't bear it...

Why did you betray Jellal?!!!

Jellal...

Wally, your voice is even louder than Shô's!

Shô!!! Keep your voice down!!!

Heh heh... Sorry, Millianna!

SLUMP

Sis, over here!!

Hurry up!!

Chapter 78:
Heaven Over There

The Magic Council chamber, Era.

You're saying that the R-System still exists?!!

That's impossible!!!

BAM

You're talking about those seven towers, right? The Council took those down. Even their ruins should be gone.

...gathered vast amounts of money. Their plan was to build the R-System.

Eight years ago... A religious sect that worshiped black magic...

Unfortunately, the local investigators aren't the joking kind...

Th-They couldn't have already built it, could they?

There were eight towers. One was near the Ka Elm sea.

The Tower of Heaven!

?!

Why would anybody be working on the R-System now?

Unnn...

So...it has been built?

It isn't called the R-System.

It's called the Tower of Heaven... right?

69

It has far too great an effect on the public!! Its use could cause panic!!!

The R-System is forbidden magic!!!

Shut your mouth, Sieg!! It doesn't matter what anybody calls it!!!

Yes, I think somebody did name it that...

We don't know...who we're up against?

However, until we know who we're dealing with...

We must get it under control without delay!!!

I want the military dispatched immediately!!!

It's some mysterious man calling himself Jellal.

What?!

The force in possession of the R-System at present doesn't seem to be the old religious cult.

We have no information on him except the name.

I've never heard the name before.

?!!

Jellal?!!

Where are they?!! Where are they?!!

Perhaps Juvia and her companions are lost.

Juvia can't believe anyone would let Gray-sama's expectations down like that!

So shape up and use it!!!

We're all depending on that nose of yours!!!

Ooo...
...oooo...
...oooo...

Hey...Natsu! Are you sure this is the right direction?

So true! Who would have expected a wizard as powerful as Erza to be defeated...

I can't think of anything more pathetic!!!

Dammit!! They went and took Erza and Happy away while we were out cold!

J-Juvia begs your forgiveness!!

Gray, calm down!!

Who said she was defeated?!!

You don't know Erza!! How dare you talk like that?!!

GLARE

...the first thing about who Erza is.

When you think of it, we don't know...

They said something about being old friends of Erza's.

Tsk!!

URFF!

WHUMP

It's been eight years since that time.

We finished it ourselves.

So you really completed it?

Eight years...?

You've changed a lot in that time.

UFF!

BUMP

Move!

......

Ceremony? You mean you're going to start up the R-System?!!

What do you expect? You're the one who betrayed us, Sis.

Jellal was really mad.

The "ceremony" takes place tomorrow at noon.

You'll wait here until then.

. . . .

So it had to be you who would be the sacrifice for the ceremony!

S-Save her, Jellal...

Save Erza-chan...

You, shut up!!!

Erza!!!

Ah ha ha ha!!

It's better than facing punishment, isn't it?

SNIFF SNIFF

No food for the rest of you for three days!

But... I was scared, so I kept quiet.

That... was pretty rotten of me, huh?

Sorry about what happened back then, Sis.

The one who planned it was me.

Huh? You know what the R-System is? I didn't expect that.

What's more important is whether you know how dangerous it is to bring people back to life using the R-System.

I don't care about that.

There are no human laws when it comes to magic.

All magic leads to the decline of human civilization.

It's a forbidden magic that breaks the laws of humanity.

The Revive System.

You sacrifice one person to bring one other person back to life.

They thought of the R-System as simply a way to return the soul to the body. It was just a method of coming back to life.

But Jellal isn't like them!!

That's exactly what black wizards say. You're just like *them!!*

He is going to actually lead us to Heaven!!

...the world will be born again!!

The moment Jellal brings *that man* back to life...

"Heaven"?

And we will control that new world!!!

Gah!!!

GRO

ONK

GRANCH

GRN

GRN

GRN

GRN

SNIP

......

FAIRY TAIL

Chapter 79:
Siegrain's Decision

This room is over-flowing with cats!!!!

Cats !!!!

I always thought Erza was a beauty!

And she's never dull!

Ha ha ha...

Jellal-sama?

Or will Erza win?

Will I win?

B-But... I find myself worried about the moves the Council will make.

The game of Heaven!!

Let's enjoy this!

Life and death...Not just that but past and future as well!!

No matter who is controlling it, we must consider them an enemy!!!

We must send out the military at once!!!

The R-System ignores the rules governing human life and death.

It is forbidden magic that gives rise to dangerous thinking!!

Era...

Sieg, you...

?!

What?!!

You bleeding-heart doves!!

MURMUR

MURMUR

You people have no idea what you are talking about!!!

There is only one method left of eliminating the Tower of Heaven now, right?!!

That thing is dangerous!!!

It's too dangerous!!!

Only doves would send out a peacekeeping force!!! We need hawks here!!!

BAM

Have you calculated the damage in lives and property?! It could take out a whole country within its blast radius!!!

You're saying to use cross-dimensional destruction magic?!!

Are you out of your mind?!!

Wha—?!

Etherion is our weapon of last resort!!! It's a magic even more dangerous than the R-System!!!

There is no other weapon aside from Etherion that can take out as big a structure as the tower!!!

The Satellite Square can affect any target on Earth!!

We don't have time to waste!!! We cannot allow the R-System to be used!!!!

If only three other members vote for it, we can use Etherion.

The Council is made up of nine members.

Ultear!!! You, too?!!

I agree.

And so vote.

If we screw up, they'll be the ones in danger!!

Erza and Happy are being held prisoner!

Who cares?! Let's just rush 'em!!

There are too many lookouts.

No!!

BLUP

Besides, it's still a long way to that tower thing over there!! We don't want to be discovered this far away!!

Yes, he did.

He praised Juvia!! Not you, Juvia!!

You're serious?! Good job!!!

Juvia has found an underwater path to the lower levels of the tower.

SHH SHH

No!!! And neither can you guys!!!

Sure!

Ten minutes? Not a problem!

We'll need to swim for approximately ten minutes underwater. Can you hold your breath that long?

BLOOSH

Hooo!

By the way, who are you again?

Then place this over your heads.

GLUSH

It's oxygen surrounded by a water shell. You should be able to breathe within it.

CHLLIP

This may be dumb-looking, but it sure came in handy!!

CHLLIP

CHLLIP

CHLLLIP

So this is the tower's basement.

GLISSH

I wonder where Erza and Happy are.

SHLIPP

PLIP?

PLIP

Cut that out!!!

Juvia was sure to make yours smaller than the rest, and yet you continued to breathe. Juvia is impressed.

Are they saying, "Come on up?"

Some kind of door just opened!!!

KREE KREE KREEK

I already told you! This is a game!!

They cleared the first stage. That's all it means.

You've allowed invaders into the tower!!!

Jellal-sama!!! What are you doing?!!

Vidaldus... Are you still stressing over that?

However, we must begin the ceremony quickly! The Council is bound to discover us sooner or later!

Ha ha ha!!

It gets even more fun now!

They won't stop me.

ZZZWIP

I need two more votes!!!! Come on, there's no time!!!!

Not the scum on the Council.

FAIRY TAIL

Chapter 80: Joan of Arc

Where are you? !!!

Box man !!!!

We didn't really control the volume during the dustup downstairs. I don't think being quiet now will help much.

MRFFL!

WHOOSH

Come on!!! This is enemy headquarters !!!

Let's use our quiet voice, shall we?

Besides. It seems someone opened the door from this side.

Moved by magic remote control.

If so, it makes it even harder to figure out why the door was opened.

Juvia and her companions are most likely being watched.

!

Provoke us, hm...?

Could they be trying to provoke something?

It's clothes from the celestial world. My clothes were soaked, so I asked Cancer to bring it along.

I know it looks great on me!

SMILE

What's with that outfit of yours?

GLEAM

GLEAM

GLEAM

Oh!!! I didn't realize we had a clothes dryer walking among us!!!

GWOOOGH

I just do this, and it dries in no time.

Juvia can turn into water, so leaving her out for the moment...

...it amazes me how you guys can stand to wear your wet clothes.

SLPP SLPP

!!!

There they are!!! The invaders!!!

WHOOO

Gah!!

ZU-KAK

KAK

KAK

Bwooh !!

KAK

!!!

GWA-HOHH !!

GAKKK

These guys don't learn, huh?

WHOOSH

That boxy guy isn't going to get away with it!!!

HUFF

HUFF

What do you mean?!! Those guys made fools of us and took off! That shames the name of Fairy Tail!!!

?!!

Go home!!!!

Um... Juvia was just... Um...

TWITCH

They kidnapped Happy!!! I'm not going home with things the way they are!!!

But Erza...

Happy?

Millianna wouldn't have...

This isn't any place for you to be.

What can you know from that?!!

Right!!! Now I know!!!

I-I can't say...

?!!

So where's this Millianna guy?!!

I know that Happy is waiting for me!!!!

Let's get going after him!!!

That idiot! Running off on his own again...

H-Hey, Natsu...

Happy!!! Here I come!!!

Natsu-san!!!

DM!!!
DM!!!
DM!!!
DM!!!

SHINNNG

!!

No!!!

You're going home!!!!

I'll take responsibility to see that Natsu and Happy get back safely.

Millianna loves cats to the extreme. I doubt she would ever put Happy in danger.

Erza!!

Like we would even consider it!!!

We're coming with you, Erza!!! We couldn't stand to do less!!!

You have to get as far away from here as possible.

We're already caught up in it!! You saw Natsu, didn't you?

This is my problem.

I don't want you people caught up in it.

Erza, what is this tower?

Who is Jellal?

...you mentioned that you used to be friends with those guys.

If you don't want to say, it's okay, but...

But we're your friends now!!

116

No matter what happens, Erza, we're on your side!!

Erza...

G–Go home...

I'm sure even you have a frightened moment or two. So what's the problem?

We're offering our strength. Take it!

I wish you'd just act like you always do and tell us to follow you without a word of explanation!

SHKK

This is nothing like you, Erza!

For-
give
me.

Urk!!

...win or lose...

...will mean that the outside world will never hear from me again.

This battle...

It is a future I cannot hope to resist.

And so...

Wh-What's that supposed to mean?!

What?!

And so, while I still exist, I will tell you everything.

This building's name is the Tower of Heaven.

It is also called the R-System.

They knew that the Council and civilian law would fobid them from building the towers, so they abducted people from the surrounding areas and enslaved them as forced labor.

Revive the dead?!!

...tried to build towers that use magic to revive the dead.

More than a decade ago, a magic religious cult dedicated to Black Magic...

What?

······

When I was very small, I was put to work here as one of the slaves.

Stand up and fight !!!! Fight for freedom !!!!!

Back then, Jellal had a true sense of justice. He was everybody's leader.

He was my ideal...

We fought for freedom...

We stood up and fought to save Jellal.

FAIRY TAIL

Chapter 81: The Voice in the Darkness

Human hate
makes me grow
stronger.

What
amusing
creatures...

!!!

After all, I
am here, so
close to them...

Where
are
you?!!

...and they
go to all
the trouble
to give me
flesh.

Wh-
Who's
there?!!

You can
meet
firsthand
the God
they so
revere.

Ah, but
you are the
lucky one,
child...

Come
out where
I can see
you!!!

But it is
only your
hate that
allows you
to sense my
presence.

They
can have
all the
"faith"
they
want.

Chapter 82:
Howling at the Moon

Hey!! Look at this!!

It's a movie lacrima!!!

CHATTER
CHATTER
MURMUR
MURMUR

But...to tell you the truth, I've never seen one either.

It's like a story. They've got actors playing the people in the story, and you can see the story play out.

KATAK

What's a movie?

It's a magic lacrima crystal that has a movie recorded in it. I never thought these guys would have something like this!

Myaa? "Movie lacrima"?

Erza...
Freedom does not exist in this world!

I will...

...have to fight Jellal...

TO BE CONTINUED

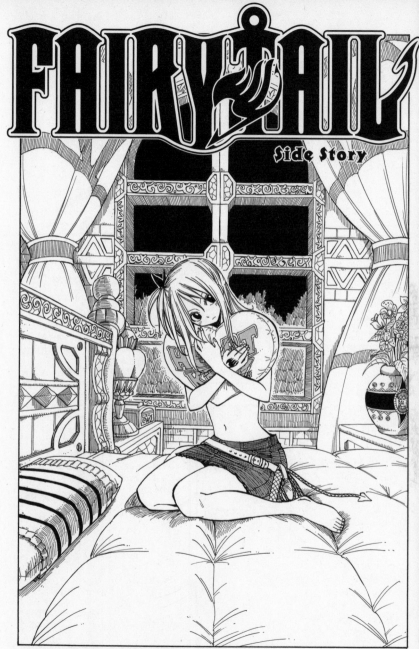

FAIRY TAIL

Side Story

Special Mission: Beware of Guys Who Show a Keen Interest

Aww!!! I've got nothing to do!!!

You should take on a job, then!

Hmm...

I don't know. It's like I'm duty bound to only go on jobs with our team.

You don't have to go with them. You could go alone or with different people.

But I told everybody else that I was going to take some time off.

Whaat?!!

You know, I think that Natsu may really like you!

It's nothing like that!!!!

You guys are so close, you could be boyfriend and girlfriend!

あっはっはっは
AH HA HA HA

The guy went like this and said, "Nin-nin!!!"

You know what happened then?!!

Nin-nin!!!

GLANCE チラ

Hey, sister! It isn't safe walking like that!!

Not a chance!!

Even if he does, I think I'll pass on that, thank you.

Honestly!! I wish Mira-san wouldn't say weird things like that!!

Aww!! I think you'd make the cutest couple!!!

Here you go again breaking into my apartment!!!!

BWAAHH

Yo!!

!!!

"Natsu may really like you!"

"Love" ...?!

What is it about my place that you love so much?

Actually, there is something very important I have to talk to you about.

G-G-G-G-Go home...

Hm?

VSH-VSH-VSH

Whoa!! Wh-What's with you?!

Go home!!!!!

What I have to say—

Oh no...

What's going on?!

B-BMP

B-BMP

B-BMP

Leave by the door!!

Geez, you're in a bad mood!

Sigh...

I've got nothing to do...

FAIRY TAIL

175

What'll I do?! What'll I do?!!

BU-BUMP

BU-BUMP

BU-BUMP

They're talking about me!!!!

He's been shouting about how he wants her!! He wants her so bad!!!

Wha?! Are we talking about the same Natsu?!!

You hear about Natsu? Word is he's totally into some girl!!

Still... I've never actually been on a date with a guy...

It isn't like I dislike him!!!

But a relationship with him or dating him isn't something I bargained for...

B-BMP

B-BMP

B-BMP

B-BMP

B-BMP

Listen, imagination!!! Don't go prettying him up without my permission!!!!

177

TWIKK

Say, Lucy...

Didn't I just tell you to cut that daydream stuff out?!!!!

There's something important I want to discuss with you tonight, okay?

Y-Yes?

SHIVER

Could you come by the Sky Tree in Southgate Park?

Wh-wh-wh-wh—

Why?

B-BMP

B-BMP

B-BMP

B-BMP

B-BMP

Later!!

BI-BI-Blushing?!! Natsu was blushing!!!!

I have something really important to say. Come alone, okay?

What'll I do?
What'll I do?!
What'll I do?!!
What'll I do?!!!

BLUB
BLUB
BLUB

There's no other explanation!!! He's about to tell me that he loves me!!!

PANIC
PANIC
PANIC
PANIC

I mean... we're on the same team and all...

I have to turn him down...

PANIC
PANIC

What'll I do?! What'll I do?!

You idiot!!!! What am I thinking?!! Stop it, me!!!

Under-wear!!!!

Is it time to wear that?!!

EBIIIIII
エビィィィ

Listen, me!!! Didn't I tell you to stop this stuff?!!!

You got it-ebi!!!

I want a cut and makeup as cute as you can make me.

SHAKII

シヤッ

IIN

シン

Hey, Lucy!!

TWITCH

Y-Yes?!!

B-BMP

B-BMP

B-BMP

B-BMP

B-BMP

Keep my cool!! That's it, just keep my cool!!!

Stay calm, Lucy!!!

I give in when they put on too much pressure!!

What'll I do?! What'll I do?!

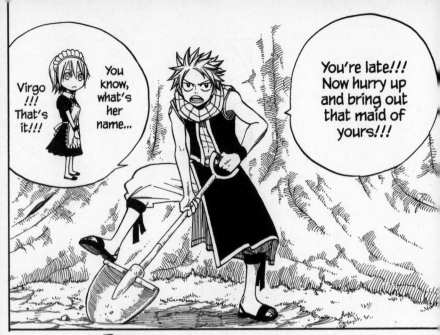

Virgo!!! That's it!!!

You know, what's her name...

You're late!!! Now hurry up and bring out that maid of yours!!!

Without that celestial spirit maid of yours, I'll never get this dug!!

GRNCH

GRNCH

This ground is way too hard!!

Huh?

They say there's treasure buried here!!

GLANCE

GLANCE

U-um...You said you had... this important thing to discuss with me...

182

It's a huge photo album of the most embarrassing pictures ever taken of the Fairy Tail members!!!

The old man hid it here a long time ago!!! Won't it be a blast to see it?!!

I don't know about "liking" her, but I do want Virgo to help me dig.

Somebody heard you say you wanted the girl so bad...

Huh?

U-Um... The rumor that you've got a girl you like...

Keeeeeeeee!!!!!

NOOOOOOOOO!!!!

SLAP

:

I am the stupidest person in the world!!!!

O....

Oww...

I...was just thinking...Gray really has a thing for you, don't you think?

Say, Lucy...

Aye?

?

I...I've decided to give up thinking.

The End

Bonus Pages

Rejected Splash Page
The pose wasn't very natural. After I noticed that, I quickly placed it in the rejected pile.

TAIL d'ART

The *Fairy Tail* Guild d'Art is an explosion of fan art! Please send in your black-and-white art on large postcard stock!! Those chosen to be published will get a signed mini poster! ♪ Make sure you write your real name and address on the back of your postcard!

▶ That's so cool! You know, you're not supposed to draw better than I can!!

Niigata Prefecture, Ai

▶ This is extremely cute!! And so well drawn!

Aomori Prefecture, Kuro

▶ What wonderful smiles!! One great piece of artwork!

Hiroshima Prefecture, MIE

▶ What did you think of the Loke story? Personally I liked it a lot.

Nagasaki Prefecture, Lemon-Sui

▶ I get lots of letters asking what became of this girl!

Miyagi Prefecture, Ikkome-chan

▶ Well done!! You've got drawing experience, don't you?

Niigata Prefecture, Reina

▶ I–I know his back-story!! R–Really! I've thought everything out!!

Yamagata Prefecture, Fuyu

▶ This is so cute!! Oh no!! I'm feeling too content!!

Kanagawa Prefecture, Mei Shimizu

FAIRY GUILD

Send to Hiro Mashima, Kodansha Comics
451 Park Ave. South, 7th Floor, New York, NY 10016

▲ It's Mira-chan from long ago! I'm getting the itch to tell that story.

By sending in letters or postcards you give us permission to give your name, address, postal code and any other information you include to the author as is. Please keep that in mind.

◄ I like her expression and pose! Petite and sexy!

Gifu Prefecture, Yasuyo Hayasaka

Miyagi Prefecture, Aoi

Rejection Corner

Osaka, Yûki Inoue

His name is Alfred DeCom. Beatrice to him.

Hiroshima Prefecture, Tabinosuke

◄ This Natsu is pretty wild, huh?

▲ This picture has an interesting flavor. What's that in the bottom left....?

Wakayama Prefecture, Buguo

Okayama Prefecture, Arashi ♡

◄ That's amazingly cute!! I love this kind of picture!!

Shiga Prefecture, Ami Horii

▲ Everybody's in animal costumes!! But Happy doesn't need a costume!

DANDY HARD

Winner of the Best Picture Macademy Award!!

Three Bullets for Tomorrow
Big Don of Arashino

I Ain't in Love

Golmon Pepes

Lexer Zorno

The True Dandy Can Cross Time Itself!!!

Story:

One hundred million jewels have been stolen from his boss, and Sharley (Golmon) chases it all the way back to the Middle Ages. But the man waiting for him there is his old friend, Tony-Joe (Lexer)!! Two men fated to battle through time! The mafia vs. the knight in this one-of-a-kind final battle!! At last, this Macademy Award—winning epic comes to a lacrima crystal near you!!!

Happy's Little Job

REQUEST BOARD

I'm Happy!!

I can't do the really tough jobs, but if there's easy work, I go solo on those jobs sometimes.

Ah!! Hey, Mr. Delivery Man!!

This time, my assignment is to see that a package is delivered!!!

Don't you think that the client who sent the request asked a wizard guild to deliver it because it's too important for regular home delivery?

Does that count as taking a job?

Sure.

Could you deliver this for me?

The End

AFTERWORD

In this volume, we plunge right into the Erza story!! You know, it's kind of hard to get the balance between the heavy dramatic stuff and the fun stuff! I try to get even a small laugh at least once into every chapter, but really, these dramatic scenes truly get in the way! This series of episodes is extremely heavy, but upon second reading, there were a lot more fun scenes than I expected (sweat sweat)!

By the way, does anybody have any guesses why there are butterflies when we first go into Erza's flashback scenes? Actually this was left over from an idea that was rejected. Does anybody out there know of the Chinese story, "The Dream of the Butterfly"?

> One day, there was a man who dreamed that he was a butterfly. When he awakened, an odd thought struck him. Could it be that my life as a butterfly was real? That I am not a man dreaming that I am a butterfly, but...

I was thinking of using a plot like that. That the present Erza is actually just the young Erza's dream of the future. Or something to that effect. But if I were to use that idea for real, what would happen to Natsu and Lucy and everybody else?! And I thought about it for a few weeks, and now the idea can only be found in those remnants. Keeping it would have made the story very complicated!

Also, there is a one other secret that's part of this episode. It's a very mean-spirited, evil plot (ha ha)! Those in the know will know what I'm talking about! And those who don't will have the enjoyment of watching the whole thing unfold. It will all become clear in volume 11...or maybe volume 12? Any of you who were fooled should scream out the words as follows:

"Mashima, you meanie!!!"

And I'll give you my answer in advance,

"I'm sorry!!"

About the Creator

HIRO MASHIMA was born May 3, 1977, in Nagano Prefecture. His series *Rave Master* has made him one of the most popular manga artists in America. *Fairy Tail*, currently being serialized in *Weekly Shônen Magazine*, is his latest creation.

Translation Notes

Japanese is a tricky language for most Westerners, and translation is often more art than science. For your edification and reading pleasure, here are notes on some of the places where we could have gone in a different direction in our translation of the work, or where a Japanese cultural reference is used.

General Notes:
Wizard

In the original Japanese version of *Fairy Tail*, you'll find panels in which the English word "wizard" is part of the original illustration. So this translation has taken that as its inspiration and translated the word *madōshi* as "wizard." But *madōshi*'s meaning is similar to certain Japanese words that have been borrowed by the English language, such as judo (the soft way) and kendo (the way of the sword). *Madō* is the way of magic, and *madōshi* are those who follow the way of magic. So although the word "wizard" is used in the original dialogue, a Japanese reader would be likely to think not of traditional Western wizards such as Merlin or Gandalf, but of martial artists.

Names

Hiro Mashima has graciously agreed to provide official English spellings for just about all of the characters in *Fairy Tail*. Because this version of *Fairy Tail* is the first publication of most of these spellings, there will inevitably be differences between these spellings and some of the fan interpretations that may have spread throughout the Web or in other fan circles. Rest assured that the spellings contained in this book are the spellings that Mashima-sensei wanted for *Fairy Tail*.

Dream of a Butterfly, page 3

The story that Mashima-sensei notes in his Afterword is a retelling of a story told in a book by the ancient Chinese philosopher Zhuangzi (also known as Chuang Tzu, 369–286 BC), who is considered to be one of the two greatest philosophers of Daoism. While Confucianism was based on self-sacrifice and conformity, the Daoism of Zhuangzi was the opposite, based on individual freedoms and escape from society and its pressures. Zhuangzi encouraged spontaneous behavior and thought, since he believed that such was a reaction to reality as it truly is, rising above societal and linguistic limitations.

Smashing Watermelons on the Beach, page 10

This is a traditional summer game for children in Japan. Like piñata games, the player is blindfolded and given a stick. Unlike a piñata, the watermelon is left sitting on the sand (or on a blanket on the sand) so Natsu's direction of "up" would make no sense. Once the watermelon is smashed, all the children divide up the watermelon pieces and eat it.

Dandy, page 20

There are many words that make their way from English into Japanese and get their meanings changed along the way. The word "dandy" doesn't mean the same in Japanese as its present English definition of a fop or a shallow, fashion-obsessed man. One Japanese dictionary starts off its definition with "a real gentleman." That is probably what Mashima-sensei was thinking when he wrote Wally's character. Since Wally got the word from the lacrima crystal movie Dandy Hard, I couldn't use "gentleman" or any other English word that might more closely indicate the Japanese meaning.

Get it?, page 23

This is an approximation rather than a translation. In Japanese, Wally uses the sentence ending particle ze at the end of most of his sentences. The way Wally uses the particle is the same way men use it when they are trying to act tough — like in the yakuza or in a street gang. The "get it" in English sounds a little like the tough character that Wally wants to be.

Big Sis, page 26

Readers of the manga *School Rumble* will be familiar with the Japanese honorific *nee-san* (or *Onee-san*), which is used by younger siblings when referring to their older sister. However, this honorific can also be used by people who are unrelated to the "big sister," such as children talking to an older girl or shop clerks who want to address a young lady but don't know her name. In *School Rumble*, the honorific appears all of the time. But here, only Shô uses it, so I decided to translate it rather than leave the honorific in Japanese.

Are you pumped up?, page 36

This was kind of difficult to translate. This is a slightly unusual phrase in Japanese that Millianna used that means about the same thing as "Are you at top energy?" But it's also similar to the standard Japanese question, *O-genki desu ka*, which basically means, "How are you?" I had to come up with a distinctive phrase that could be Millianna's catchphrase without losing the meaning of the original. "Are you pumped up?" seemed like a good compromise.

-ebi, page 102

As explained in the notes for volume 2, some manga and anime characters end their sentences with small, meaningless syllables that are distinctive to the character. In Japanese children's stories, crabs usually end their sentences with *-kani* (*kani* means "crab" in Japanese). But although Cancer is a crab, he ends his sentences with *-ebi* (*ebi* means "shrimp" in Japanese). It was a little joke in volume 2, but it has also become a part of Cancer's character.

With Kase-sensei!

Weekly Shônen Magazine is celebrating its fiftieth birthday!!! And as part of the festivities, I get to draw a manga that is a tribute to Kase-sensei's manga, *Chameleon*. This is a picture of when I conferred with him. I think it's pretty incredible to be able to be in the same photo as a manga-ka that I've admired ever since my student days! And that thought was keenly felt throughout the entire interview. Even so, Kase-sensei is a fun guy! But that's only natural since the most interesting manga come from interesting people, huh?

—Hiro Mashima

Honorifics Explained

Throughout the Kodansha Comics books, you will find Japanese honorifics left intact in the translations. For those not familiar with how the Japanese use honorifics and, more important, how they differ from American honorifics, we present this brief overview.

Politeness has always been a critical facet of Japanese culture. Ever since the feudal era, when Japan was a highly stratified society, use of honorifics—which can be defined as polite speech that indicates relationship or status—has played an essential role in the Japanese language. When addressing someone in Japanese, an honorific usually takes the form of a suffix attached to one's name (example: "Asuna-san"), is used as a title at the end of one's name, or appears in place of the name itself (example: "Negi-sensei," or simply "Sensei").

Honorifics can be expressions of respect or endearment. In the context of manga and anime, honorifics give insight into the nature of the relationship between characters. Many English translations leave out these important honorifics and therefore distort the feel of the original Japanese. Because Japanese honorifics contain nuances that English honorifics lack, it is our policy at Kodansha not to translate them. Here, instead, is a guide to some of the honorifics you may encounter in Kodansha Comics.

-**san:**   This is the most common honorific and is equivalent to Mr., Miss, Ms., or Mrs. It is the all-purpose honorific and can be used in any situation where politeness is required.

-**sama:**   This is one level higher than "-san" and is used to confer great respect.

-**dono:**   This comes from the word "tono," which means "lord." It is an even higher level than "-sama" and confers utmost respect.

-kun: This suffix is used at the end of boys' names to express familiarity or endearment. It is also sometimes used by men among friends, or when addressing someone younger or of a lower station.

-chan: This is used to express endearment, mostly toward girls. It is also used for little boys, pets, and even between lovers. It gives a sense of childish cuteness.

Bozu: This is an informal way to refer to a boy, similar to the English terms "kid" and "squirt."

Sempai/
Senpai: This title suggests that the addressee is one's senior in a group or organization. It is most often used in a school setting, where underclassmen refer to their upperclassmen as "sempai." It can also be used in the workplace, such as when a newer employee addresses an employee who has seniority in the company.

Kohai: This is the opposite of "sempai" and is used toward underclassmen in school or newcomers in the workplace. It connotes that the addressee is of a lower station.

Sensei: Literally meaning "one who has come before," this title is used for teachers, doctors, or masters of any profession or art.

-[blank]: This is usually forgotten in these lists, but it is perhaps the most significant difference between Japanese and English. The lack of honorific means that the speaker has permission to address the person in a very intimate way. Usually, only family, spouses, or very close friends have this kind of permission. Known as *yobisute*, it can be gratifying when someone who has earned the intimacy starts to call one by one's name without an honorific. But when that intimacy hasn't been earned, it can be very insulting.

Preview of Volume 11

We're pleased to present you with a preview from volume 11, now available from Kodansha Comics. Check out our Web site (www.kodanshacomics.com) for more details!

Meeting Place of the Magic Council: Era...

We have to wipe the Tower of Heaven off the face of the Earth!

We have to be sure that Jellal cannot use the R-System!!!

And the only possible way available to us is to attack the tower using the Satellite Square, Etherion!!!

The R-System is a forbidden magic of which all records must be obliterated from history.

Hm...

But...

I'm sure you all know what that means.

Every living being within that tower will be wiped out!!

That includes any humans in the area!

Everything that falls under the Etherion attack is rendered "null!"

It is a price we must pay!

This is to protect the entire magic world!

In a manner of speaking, we ourselves will be one of those sacrifices.

Elder Belno!!

SKRRT

Elder Leiji!! If we make an unannounced attack on Ka-Elm national soil, history will record *our names* on the list of mass murderers!!!

It is exactly as Sieg says. We live now only because others have previously sacrificed their lives. The history of magic proves that over and over.

CHATTER

I see no alternative! I agree to use Etherion.

What?!!

We must say that to the children when we teach them of the sanctity of human life!

"The dead cannot be brought back to life!"

CHATTER

Only one more vote... hm?

We need only one more vote!!

No... just talking to myself.

Did you say something, Jellal-sama?

Sir?

202

Only one more until game over.

Heh heh heh...

Yes... The legendary black wizard, known as the greatest evil in the history of the magical world.

That Zeref that you mentioned...

Wait a second, Erza...

That isn't all. It's probably that Deliora is also a demon from the Book of Zeref.

Wh-When the demon came out of Lullaby, didn't somebody say something about the Book of Zeref?

!!!

So Jellal is trying to revive this Zeref?

They say that Zeref had enough magic power to easily create frightening creatures like those.

Shô...

Some of my old friends say that when Zeref is resurrected, he could become ruler in heaven, or something like that.

I don't understand his motive.

They were saying that you betrayed them, Erza...

...but wasn't it really Jellal who betrayed them?

Now that you mention it, there's one thing I don't understand about your old friends.

However, I abandoned them for eight years.

There is little difference between that and a direct betrayal.

Perhaps he indoctrinated them somehow after he expelled me from the Tower of Heaven.

But that's only because Jellal threatened your friends' lives if you ever even got close!!

And even then, he—

That's enough, Lucy.

If I am able to defeat Jellal, then it will all be over.

SHK

...will mean that the outside world will never hear from me again.

This battle... ...win or lose...

For some reason, those words keep coming back to me.

I wonder if that's really true.

A Kodansha Comics trade Paperback Original

Fairy Tail volume 10 copyright © 2008 Hiro Mashima
English translation copyright © 2010 Hiro Mashima

Published in the United States by Kodansha Comics, an imprint of Kodansha USA Publishing, LLC., New York.

Publication rights for this English edition arranged through Kodansha Ltd., Tokyo.

First published in Japan in 2008 by Kodansha Ltd., Tokyo

ISBN 978-1-612-62281-1

Printed in the United States of America

www.kodanshacomics.com

9 8 7

Translator/Adapter: William Flanagan
Lettering: North Market Street Graphics

TOMARE!

[STOP!]

You're going the wrong way!

Manga is a completely different type of reading experience.

To start at the *beginning*, go to the *end*!

That's right! Authentic manga is read the traditional Japanese way—from right to left, exactly the *opposite* of how American books are read. It's easy to follow: Just go to the other end of the book and read each page—and each panel—from right side to left side, starting at the top right. Now you're experiencing manga as it was meant to be!

Listen up, guys! This is the table of contents for *Fairy Tail 10!*

FAIRY TAIL

10

HIRO MASHIMA